The Essential Charles Bruce

The Essential Charles Bruce

selected by Carmine Starnino

The Porcupine's Quill

Library and Archives Canada Cataloguing in Publication

Bruce, Charles, 1906–1971
[Poems. Selections]
The essential Charles Bruce / selected by Carmine Starnino.

(Essential poets series ; 18)
Poems.
Includes bibliographical references.
ISBN 978-0-88984-416-2 (softcover)

I. Starnino, Carmine, editor II. Title. III. Series: Essential poets series ; 18

PS8503.R91A6 2018 C811'.52 C2018-903919-1

1 2 3 • 20 19 18

Published by The Porcupine's Quill, 68 Main Street, PO Box 160, Erin, Ontario NOB 1TO. http://porcupinesquill.ca

Represented in Canada by Canadian Manda.
Trade orders are available from University of Toronto Press.

We acknowledge the support of the Ontario Arts Council and the Canada Council for the Arts for our publishing program. The financial support of the Government of Canada is also gratefully acknowledged.

Canada Council for the Arts Conseil des arts du Canada
ONTARIO ARTS COUNCIL
CONSEIL DES ARTS DE L'ONTARIO
an Ontario government agency
un organisme du gouvernement de l'Ontario
Canada
Ontario
Ontario Media Development Corporation

Table of Contents

Foreword

Fifty-two years ago, the Governor General's Award for Poetry was given to a collection that took as its subject a quiet, cast-aside stretch of Nova Scotia called Chedabucto Bay. The poet, a newspaperman named Charles Bruce, had spent his boyhood along the north shore of that bay, and the book, called *The Mulgrave Road,* conveyed the maritime details of those early experiences in clear, direct, metrical verse — verse Bruce described as 'simple and stirring and understandable without drifting into banality, using the concrete terms of life.'

Not exactly the credo of a trend-watcher, and indeed that sort of throwback thinking, uttered during Canada's modernist heyday, conferred on Bruce's career a certain fustiness. One reviewer, unhappy with *The Mulgrave Road*'s 'local colour', complained that it comprised 'trite universals which meet on the fair-weather ground of inadequate and uninspired words' and another groused that the poetry 'reaches into the backwaters which the busy world has bypassed'. Bruce had fans, of course. Frye praised the collection as 'consistently successful' and A.J.M. Smith included Bruce's poems in his *Oxford Book of Canadian Verse,* as did Ralph Gustafson in his own *Penguin Book of Canadian Verse.* But Bruce's small-scale, regional lyricism kept him to one side of the country's poetical developments, and the fact that he dedicated himself to this outsiderism — proudly regarding his poems as an alternative to the 'whole academic approach to poetry' which he called 'an irritant' — certainly didn't help.

After his death in 1971, Bruce drifted famelessly out of mind, and nowadays dropping his name into a literary conversation will fetch you a blank look. In the mid-eighties Andy Wainwright made a yeoman's effort of championing him, penning a literary biography and editing, with Leslie Choyce, a volume of his selected poems (both out of print). But aside from an essay in the autumn 1979 issue of *The Dalhousie Review,* Bruce's poetry has attracted zero scholarship, and he now survives — barely — as a regional curiosity. I certainly had no clue of his existence until my friend Michael Harris picked up *The Mulgrave Road* (for ten cents!) during a Saturday-morning visit to a Westmount estate sale. He invited me over to his home that afternoon. He was excited, and this, called 'Biography', is what he read to me:

> His speckled pastures dipped to meet the beach
> Where the old fish huts stood. At his front door
> A man could stand and see the whole wide reach
> Of blue Atlantic. But he stayed ashore.
>
> He stayed ashore and plowed, and drilled his rows,
> And planned his hours and finished what he planned.
> And made his profits: colts and calves and ewes
> And buildings and piled stone and harrowed land.
>
> He was a careful man, a trifle cold
> To meet and talk to. There were some who thought
> His hand was a bit grasping, when he sold;
> A little slow to open when he bought.
>
> But no one said it that way. When you heard
> His habits mentioned, there would be a pause.
> And then the soft explanatory word.
> They said he was dry-footed. And he was.

Hearing these lines, I was struck by their plain-talking directness—so plain, in fact, they hardly seemed poetry at all. I've since read 'Biography' dozens of times, and always I marvel at the resourcefulness Bruce brought to its simplicity of parts (the third stanza, for instance, is held together entirely by a deft, end-stopping repetition of 'and'). The poem seems to me perfectly played. It knows from the start where it's headed, joins the right details to the right diction, and has them stop at the right time, on the right clean note. It's hard not to consider the poem's clarity, concision and higher artlessness as a happy carry-over from the 'clear and crisp copy' of Bruce's newspaper writing.

But however much we may appreciate the efficiency of stanza and rhyme—the thousand tiny adjustments carried out to snugly bed the yarn-spinning, cracker-barrel voice inside a tightly organized structure—we will misunderstand the poem, I believe, if we miss the fact that running through the voice, keeping warm just under its flinty surface, is a suggestion of suspicion. Add up 'a trifle cold', 'a bit grasping', 'a little slow' and you realize that the speaker is hintingly delivering his distrust of dry-footedness.

Chedabucto Bay was home to both farmers and fishermen, and the tension between the territory's earth-reekers and its sea-workers (explored elsewhere in *The Mulgrave Road*) gives the poem its larger theatre. All this is enough, in my opinion, to make 'Biography' a contemporary classic. With its spontaneity of speech ('But he stayed ashore. // He stayed ashore and plowed'), its pithy phrasings ('There were some who thought / His hand was a bit grasping'), its abrupt surprises ('But no one said it that way') and its gossipy, slightly insinuating tinctures ('When you heard / His habits mentioned, there would be a pause. / And then the soft explanatory word.') the poem tries to capture the gradient of a particular life by capturing the inflections of a particular vernacular.

The lovely effect of that effort — the sound of a human voice working inside the sound of a poem — calls up Seamus Heaney. Heaney, like Bruce, is also a practitioner of the homespun dialect. But the poet I'm reminded of most by this casual, somewhat countrified accent is the poet in whose work Heaney himself first heard it: Frost. Here's another example:

Cleaning fish is a job you would balk at;
But nothing is mean with gulls hovering down,
Sun brighter than life on glistening eelgrass,
The bay crawling again in a quickening southwest wind.

There was always a time after the wash barrels were empty,
After hand-barrows were lugged up the beach to the hut,
And herring lay behind handwrought staves, clean with salt —

Time to lie on warm stone and listen
While the sting went out of crooked fingers and thighs ceased to ache;
Time to hear men's voices, coming quietly through a coloured cloth of sound
Woven in the slap of water on fluent gravel.
Their talk was slow and quiet, of fish and men
And fields back on the hill with fences down,
Hay to be made through long hot days with never a splash on the oilskins,
Or the lift of water awake under half-inch pine.

Like Frost's, Bruce's aesthetic is that of the spoken cadence. The poem has that supple, pellucid feel we like to think of as a trait of a 'natural' voice. Bruce evokes this by using, as in 'Biography', a large number of one- and two-syllable words (in fact I think of this as the same speaker, now giving us the other side of the story) and by straightforwardly sinking his details into the conversational texture of his lines. Note, especially, the laid-back fluency with which Bruce strikes off his phrases: 'Cleaning fish is a job you would balk at', 'Sun brighter than life on glistening eelgrass', 'fields back on the hill with fences down' or 'a coloured cloth of sound / Woven in the slap of water on fluent gravel' with the finely judged double meaning of 'fluent' (and doesn't the image look forward to Heaney's 'Bluebottles / Wove a strong gauze of sound around the smell'?)

This sort of poetry—alert, unfussy, brisk, convincingly thrown—is nearly impossible to find before Bruce. In his *Dalhousie* essay, Richard C. Davis argues for Charles G.D. Roberts as Bruce's turn-of-the-century tutelary spirit. There is, to be sure, a shared bucolic imagery and setting, but there's nothing in Roberts that could have helped Bruce forge poems so dependent on the acoustics of a speaking voice. Roberts's best descriptive lines ('A brown, sad-coloured hillside, where the soil / Fresh from the frequent harrow, deep and fine, / Lies bare') can't compete with the observational intensity of 'Hay to be made through long hot days with never a splash on the oilskins, / Or the lift of water awake under half-inch pine.'

The ear that arrived at 'awake' is what I'm celebrating here; how that word brings an impulsiveness to Bruce's description, surprising the line with its colloquial bite. *The Mulgrave Road* thus introduced to Canadian poetry one of the most convincing examples of what Tom Paulin calls the 'vernacular imagination'. The poems welcome a specific region of the country into the personifying range of their lyric consciousness, converting geographical space to vocal property. It's a major achievement, and Bruce's most valuable contribution to our literature. Listen to the ending of 'Nova Scotia Fish Hut' where we can, again, catch Bruce at work charting Chedabucto Bay's linguistic self-definition:

> Wait if you like: someone will come to find
> A handline or a gutting-knife, or stow

A coiled net in the loft. Or just to smoke
And loaf; and swap tomorrow in slow talk;
And knock his pipe out on a killick-rock
Someone left lying sixty years ago.

Here are six simple, iambically clean lines fitted with unspectacular data. All in all, a modest moment. Bruce's best poems, however, are composed entirely of such modest moments, with each of them, like this one, thriving inside their ordinary, workaday music. Consider the words 'Wait if you like'. It seems like an ordinary phrase, no? But with it the Robertsian legacy of ritualized, hallowed eloquence is brought up short. With it — and with hundreds of instances like it in *The Mulgrave Road* — Bruce unsublimes Canadian pastoral poetry into something rougher, accidental-seeming and homemade in its effects.

True, Roberts had also sought to scuff the world into a commonplace colour, but he was unable finally to stay away from richer, more artificial pigments. Roberts's landscapes always have a poeticized pageantry to them: 'From fence to fence a perfumed breath exhales / O'er the bright pallor of the well-loved fields', 'I hear the low wind wash the softening snow', 'Skirting the sunbright uplands stretches a riband of meadow, / Shorn of the labouring grass'. Now compare those lines to the impromptu naturalness of 'Wait if you like' — captured, as Frost would put it, fresh from talk. The phrase feels direct and unpretending, not well-groomed and official, as does the rest of the voice that immediately presses ahead with the task of cataloguing such humble objects as 'handline', 'gutting-knife', 'coiled net', 'pipe'.

Notice, as well, the assonantal terseness and monosyllabic muscularity of Bruce's vocabulary: stow/smoke/talk/knock/rock or knife/net/loft/loaf/left. It's one thing to pretend to not be above such mundane details, as Roberts did, but it's quite another to determinedly level your diction to meet those details. In other words, unlike Roberts, there's nothing prissy about Bruce. And if the lines seem merely a matter-of-fact staking out of a scene, one should keep in mind that it is matter-of-fact in a way that was, then, remarkable. It is matter-of-fact in the way that opts for vernacular genuineness over refined perfectionism. It is matter-of-fact in a way that rejects smooth, Tennysonian tunes and favours the square-shouldered taciturn cadences found in the language used by the men Bruce knew — a drawl you can hear in 'Eastern Shore':

> He stands and walks as if his knees were tensed
> To a pitching dory. When he looks far off
> You think of trawl-kegs rolling in the trough
> Of swaying waves. He wears a cap against
> The sun on water, but his face is brown
> As an old mainsail, from the eyebrows down.

We are now very far from Pauline Johnson's 'And like a spirit, swathed in some soft veil, / Steals twilight and its shadows o'er the swale' or Marjorie Pickthall's 'Thoughts sweet as flowers / Linger for hours'. There is a masculine severity to the first stanza of 'Eastern Shore'. This is poetry as a form of tough talk, poetry with a certain man's man technical prowess (even the rhyming of 'off' with 'trough' has a kind of hard-bitten satisfaction to it). The terrific use of 'tensed' — with the raw embodying energy that verb brings to the image — is the result of a pledge between physical sensation and vocal stress, between the world as lived and the language as spoken. This was a pledge largely missing in Canadian poetry, which could manufacture sonorously stylized reports on the local and the particular, but was unable to touch off a run of sounds (as in 'trawl-kegs rolling in the trough / Of swaying waves') that could themselves comprise a convincing dialect of viscerality.

And it's with that pledge that Bruce nudged the Canadian pastoral lyric as it had been practised by the Confederation crew — Charles G.D. Roberts, Bliss Carman, Duncan Campbell Scott, Archibald Lampman — into an entirely new region of realness. Compare Campbell Scott's 'Sometimes a titan wind, slumberous and hushed, / Takes the dark grove within his swinging power' to Bruce's 'The wind goes washing through high trees / Remotely, with a sound of seas'. The successful tactility of Bruce's image is secured not merely with his eye but with his ear. All of Bruce's descriptions are similarly countersunk in sound.

Or take the ending to 'Tidehead' (p. 46): 'Enough to have seen — / The marsh a moist blotter, / And the slick wet green / Of eelgrass at low water'. Bruce's auditory imagination flexes itself here in the subtlest ways, generating a small, sensuous wind that blows a wetness into the words. While Bruce's oeuvre includes many portraits of farmers and fishermen, the standard touchstones of his verse — rocks, cliffsides, hills, shores, beaches, wind and tides — are as mesmerically drawn as the characters who live and work among them. His idiom, in other words, implicates itself in the actions and turnings of maritime landscape and weather; the poems in *The Mulgrave Road* can thus be understood as another expression of the densities of sea, sand and soil:

Back Road Farm

This house is built within a sheltering
Sweep of the hills. You will not find the sea
From attic windows; and the seasons bring
No lift and change of tide, here in the lee
Of the land's high windbreak, where the buffeting
Onshore wind is tripped on the mountain's knee.
No mist of blowing salt is flung to sting
The trusting flesh. You will not find the sea.

This property is private. Drifting rain
Beats on its shingles and its native stone;
The wind of August on its leaning grain
Is dark with shadow, and the leaves are blown
To a soft thunder. But the hills remain;
Their strength is certain and their purpose known.
Only at night, in the stillness, low and plain
You can hear the far deep rumor of sea on stone.

Now, think. It's 1951 and Canada's poetical air is thick with hermeticism, proto-philosophical poses, metaphysical wit and mythologizing. Who else is writing poems like 'Back Road Farm' — poems with such a gruff, low-colloquial burr? Irving Layton? Leonard Cohen? F.R. Scott maybe? How about A.J.M. Smith, P.K. Page, Anne Wilkinson? All are wonderful poets, but each was consumed by what Heaney once called 'mind-stuff', for whom a topic as parochial as a farmhouse would have needed a little elucidatory brightening, some extra attention-holding airbrushing.

Bruce's poems, however, embodied no large-scale aesthetic theory, refused to serve as a subset of a political ideology, didn't give voice to the unconscious, weren't premised on any hidden-away allusions, had no esoteric range of reference and wanted nothing to do with obscurity. Bruce instead believed in writing poetry where 'expression is disciplined by sticking to a person's own observation of the way a spike-tooth harrow scrawls across a field.' Indifferent to the schools and counterschools of modernism's two great campaigns (the embrace of the urban, the urbane and the ironic; or the plunge into the chthonic, the subconscious and the vatic), Bruce's poems display the practical, no-nonsense thinking of a man who remained, at heart, a Chedabucto Bay boy, loyal to tribe and dialect. 'Keats' famous phrase about truth and beauty is merely a quotable cliché,' Bruce once wrote. 'There is no such thing as abstract truth or abstract beauty ... there are simply acts, words, people, scenes that strike you with conviction or recognition.'

The poems in *The Mulgrave Road*—and the 'acts, words, people, scenes' they turn on—may seem too low-key in intention to be interested in staking great claims; nonetheless, when reintroduced into their historical context, these same poems (poems, as one reviewer put it, 'unscarred by fad or oddity') are voltaged with literary daring. In order to appreciate Bruce's exciting delinquency in concentrating on common things, one needs to appreciate that his two working principles—that poems should sound like talk, and to evoke is better than to say—did more than bring a tremendous conviction of tone to his lines: they redressed modernism's withdrawal from a living, immediate, vernacular audience.

Bruce wrote the following passage in 1953 in a letter to Frye (he was replying to Frye's favourable review of *The Mulgrave Road*):

> What happens in the creation of poetry is that the poet realizes a set of circumstances, involving all sorts of things—people, building, landscapes, events—which cause in him a certain excitement. He doesn't say 'These things make me feel so-and-so.' He tries to re-create imaginatively and suggestively that set of circumstances, in the hope that through his exactitude ... he can create something like the same excitement in someone

else. That seems to me to be the whole end and method of poetry whether traditional or modern in form.

The philosophy summed up in this passage—poetry as a transference of emotional heat from poet to reader—seems a clear expression of Bruce's artistry and that artistry's public quarrel with the intellectualism of the times. It was, of course, a losing battle. In his influential 1961 survey, *Creative Writing in Canada*, Desmond Pacey—in sentences that probably flung Bruce from whatever small cliff of attention he was still clinging to—advised readers that Bruce was 'a pleasant if not particularly forceful poet' whose 'chief talents are for the description of natural scenery in a rather austere, stripped style and for a sort of gentle, relaxed introspectiveness.'

At a time when poets were celebrated for their bold contemporary thinking, Bruce cut an odd figure; old-fangled in his hayseed simplicities, a tad *vieux jeu* in his pretensions. The fact that his poems drew sustenance from the lore and legend of community kept him marginal in a period dominated by big-game theorizing. However it was exactly that backward movement toward early sources and certainties that allowed Bruce to bring to Canadian poetry an improved meshing of language and place. As with Whitman, Twain, Kipling, Hemingway and Bellow, Bruce was committed to a plain-minded language that appealed directly to the ear ('what's hard to say is hard to read') and that exploited the non-poetic poetic persuasiveness of common speech.

I believe, though, that *The Mulgrave Road* was a book chanced into being: a case of ambition discovered rather than ambition assumed. What began as a modest gambit (to recreate 'the trenchant bite / Of cold salt water') found itself playing for far more serious stakes. Its surface rusticity made *The Mulgrave Road* easy for critics like Pacey to set aside, but by building poems that gathered such a rich aural harvest of basic emotion, simple detail and accurate perception—and did so by using 'concrete nouns and moving verbs to recreate the things that woke the feeling'—Bruce helped change Canadian poetry's fundamental intuition of the beautiful, and the rhythm embodying that sense of the beautiful.

Even today, the satisfaction of reading Bruce comes from confronting many of the fundamentals we tend to forget about poetry — most importantly that it's never contrived by committee, hype or movement. Independence, for Bruce, was the one true ethic of creativity. He showed little reverence for the poetry community: its self-conscious, careerist sense of the poetic enterprise, its strived-for principles of fame. When Bruce did voice his opinions about his contemporaries, he could be scathing. He declared Klein's 'Portrait of the Poet as Landscape' to be 'as clinically revelatory as the successive coloured cut-outs in an old-fashioned "Doctor's Book"' and charged that Layton's poems were 'Lead coinage with fancy design'.

In these situations — dusting off a long-shelved career in order to put it back into general view — there's a tendency to make angry claims for the neglected talent. I regret the circumstances that kept me from learning of him sooner, but I don't see Bruce as a victim. He kept to the margins for so long the canon simply inherited his self-scripted disappearance. Also, Bruce didn't get a chance to write the poems he wanted to write — energetic, emotionally persuasive, with a rich relationship to the vernacular — until *The Mulgrave Road*. What began with the mannered melodiousness of *Wild Apples* (1927) found its way, four books and two decades later, to utterances of alliterative solidity and hard consonants, where 'shouted sound from granite-throated hills' is given back 'harsh and high, and wild with meaning' (which is itself a smaller narrative of Canadian poetry's own journey and how it discovered one of its greatest destinies in Bruce).

But by the time *The Mulgrave Road* came about, Bruce was like Hugh Currie from his own unpublished novel, *Currie Head*, who 'could handle a two-master, cut a sail, caulk a seam, clean and salt fish, knit and mend nets, and even make a spoked cartwheel, the trickiest job known to one-horse farming' but sadly 'had come to his highest proficiency just when the value of these skills was beginning to go out with the slowly turning tide.' It's time, I think, for that tide to turn back to Bruce.

Carmine Starnino
Toronto, Ontario

Biography

His speckled pastures dipped to meet the beach
Where the old fish huts stood. At his front door
A man could stand and see the whole wide reach
Of blue Atlantic. But he stayed ashore.

He stayed ashore and plowed, and drilled his rows,
And planned his hours and finished what he planned.
And made his profits: colts and calves and ewes
And buildings and piled stone and harrowed land.

He was a careful man, a trifle cold
To meet and talk to. There were some who thought
His hand was a bit grasping, when he sold;
A little slow to open when he bought.

But no one said it that way. When you heard
His habits mentioned, there would be a pause.
And then the soft explanatory word.
They said he was dry-footed. And he was.

Words Are Never Enough

These are the fellows who smell of salt to the prairie,
Keep the back country informed of crumbling swell
That buckles the international course off Halifax
After a night of wind:
Angus Walters and Ben Pine, carrying on for Tommy Himmelman and
Marty Welch,
Heading up the tough men who get into the news,
Heading up the hard men of Lunenberg and Gloucester,
Keeping the cities bordered with grass and grain
Forever mindful that something wet and salt
Creeps and loafs and marches round the continent,
Careless of time, careless of change, obeying the moon.

Listen to little Angus, squinting at the Bluenose:
'The timber that'll beat her still stands in the woods.'
Yes, these are the fellows who remind you again of the sea.

But one town, or two,
Are never enough to keep salt in the blood.

I haven't seen Queensport Light over the loom of Ragged Head
    in years,
And never a smell of rollers coming up the bay from Canso.
No one ever heard of Queensport outside of a bait report;
No one ever saw the name of Ragged Head anywhere.

Off that obscure beach, Will Bruce and George McMaster
Set their herring nets, and went further out for mackerel.

The mackerel never ran, but in July
Fat herring tangled in wet twine were silver-thick,
And the flat low in the water as we hauled around
to head back for the huts;
In full daylight now,
After the grey dusk of windless morning;
After the bay, gently stirring in half darkness,
Tapped down again to blush at the sun's rim.

Cleaning fish is a job you would balk at;
But nothing is mean with gulls hovering down,
Sun brighter than life on glistening eelgrass,
The bay crawling again in a quickening southwest wind.

There was always a time after the wash barrels were empty,
After hand-barrows were lugged up the beach to the hut,
And herring lay behind handwrought staves, clean with salt—

Time to lie on warm stone and listen
While the sting went out of crooked fingers and thighs ceased
to ache;
Time to hear men's voices, coming quietly through a coloured cloth
of sound
Woven in the slap of water on fluent gravel.

Their talk was slow and quiet, of fish and men
And fields back on the hill with fences down,
Hay to be made through long hot days with never a splash on the
oilskins,
Or the lift of water awake under half-inch pine.

The mackerel never rain, and if the herring
had been only a story, a legend for midnight telling,
These would have launched their flats and tended the empty nets.

I know it now, remembering now the calm;
Remembering now the lowering care that lifted
From a face turned to the wind off Ragged Head.

These are the fellows who keep salt in the blood.
Knowing it fresh in themselves, needful as hope,
They give to the cities bordered with woods and grass
a few homesick men, walking an alien street;
A few women, remembering misty stars
And the long grumbling sight of the bay at night.

Words are never enough; these are aware
Somewhere deep in the soundless well of knowing,
That sea, in the flesh and nerves and the puzzling mind
Of children born to the long grip of its tide,
Must always wash the land's remotest heart.
These are the fellows who keep salt in the blood.

Islands

Islands are a different country. Something more
Than straits and channels and the sweep of sea
Divides their beaches from the blunted shore.
Some island thing, in moss and grass and tree,
Nursed by the wind and rooted in grey rock,
Stubborn as time and sharp as winter thorn—
And something in the look and step and talk
And touch of men and women, island born.
An absent look, a listening in the eyes.
As if they heard, in blood and flesh and bone,
Between the breakers' rise and fall and rise
Some word let fall between the sea and stone.
    But never ask me what. How should I know?
    I was born inland. Half a mile or so.

The Independent

His precept was that every tub should stand
On its own bottom. Let the thing be done
By strength and purpose, by your own hard hand.
He asked no help and he would proffer none.

That was the way he was. A man of pride;
A man of strength and substance; hard and grim
And independent till the day he died.
He died alone. The neighbours buried him.

Wave

Something far out far off under asian cloud
No line no limit but the invisible curve
In a theorem of sea and sky,
And no eye there to see no mind to prove it—
Wind brushed that fluent sleep.

Wind from the planes
The cold euclidean steppes ...

Shiver and stir. Ripple and flaw. Clouded stillness
Darkens where the invisible wind curls up
The waking wave.

Ripple and ridge. Curtsy and dip and lop ...
Out from the puppet-shift and sway and stir
The quick dancer walks.

The dancer. Walking. Till the stilted walk
Steadies
And rolls
And leagued in rolling seas the combers come
Wind-driven in a thousand miles of fetch.

Sombre and towering now the ridge, the windscrawl—
That slopes and forms and follows and casts back
Self after fluent self.
Only the form eternal (while the wind holds),
The flowing shape through sea and sea and sea ...
Until at last self shape one moment one
Break
On the asking granite of the shore.

Nova Scotia Fish Hut

Rain and blown sand, and southwest wind
Have rubbed these shingles crisp and paper-thin.
Come in:
Something has stripped these studding-posts and pinned
Time to the rafters. Where the woodworm ticked
Shick shick shick shick
Steady and secretive, his track is plain:
The fallen bark is dust; the beams are bare.

Bare as the bare stone of this open shore,
This building grey as stone. The filtered sun
Leaks cold and quiet through it. And the rain,
The wind, the whispering sand, return to finger
Its creaking wall, and creak its thuttering door.

Old, as the shore is. But they use the place.
Wait if you like: someone will come to find
A handline or a gutting-knife, or stow
A coiled net in the loft. Or just to smoke
And loaf; and swap tomorrow in slow talk;
And knock his pipe out on a killick-rock
Someone left lying sixty years ago.

Tidewater Morning

Searching the windy strait with narrowed frown,
She finds between the wrinkled rise and fall
Of marching seas, a dory, cruising down
The channel's reach with tubs of running trawl.
His time were better spent, she knows, attending
The careful urging of her common sense:
Breaking the upper field to seed, and mending
The kitchen roof, and bracing flattened fence ...

But as he climbs the rutted pasture now,
Hungry from wind and tide, and oar and barrow—
Here heart forgets the sowing and the plow,
Meeting again the strength that never took
Its grace from gardens, and the long clear look
That never learned its blue behind a barrow.

Eastern Shore

He stands and walks as if his knees were tensed
To a pitching dory. When he looks far off
You think of trawl-kegs rolling in the trough
Of swaying waves. He wears a cap against
The sun on water, but his face is brown
As an old mainsail, from the eyebrows down.

He has grown old as something used and known
Grows old with custom; each small fading scar
Engrained by use and wear in plank and spar,
In weathered wood and iron, and flesh and bone.
But youth lurks in the squinting eyes, and in
The laughter wrinkles in the tanbark skin.

You know his story when you see him climb
The lookout hill. You know that age can be
A hill of looking; and the swaying sea
A lifetime marching with the waves of time.
Listen — the ceaseless cadence, deep and slow.
Tomorrow. Now. And years and years ago.

The Other Shore

The opposite shore was low and far, and flawed
With Asian darkness. Nothing gleamed. No stir
Of wind or tide could reach the cobalt blur
Of that dim country under the sleeping cloud.

We sailed the water once, on drumming wind.
Astern the landmarks merged and fell away.
And slowly there, across that marching sway
Of seas, the blue shore lightened ... and was land.

Far out, beyond our bowsprit's veer and swerve
The blue land livened: planes of bronze and green
Broke on the slopes unfolding there, between
The shawl of cloud and the white thread of surf.

Slowly it sharpened: hills and climbing roads,
And fields above the measured rise and fall ...
Barns, fences, houses, cattle, beetle-small
In pastures hemmed from the dark cape of woods.

Earth, rock, fields, people, were the leaf and bloom
Of that strange land. We sheltered in its lee.
And turned away and saw the whole wide sky and sea,
And low and far, the cobalt blur of home.

Immediates*

IMMEDIATES? Let us take for text
The bite of salt through sodden wool,
And place a running headrope next
Ink by the pen or bucketful.

Two cents for haddock, one for cod;
Weather a chance, and wind a guess —
But no allegiance to the god
Of unavailing bitterness.

Here on the roofless beach they know
The fallibility of plan,
That justice and injustice grow
Not from system but the man.

An ageless land and sea conspire
To smooth the imperfect mould of birth;
While freezing spray and drying fire
Translate the inexplicit earth.

'Get understanding first of these:
The open cut, the healing scar;
Before you flick prophetic keys
To tell us what immediates are.'

* In 1936 Leo Kennedy wrote in *New Frontier*: 'Bruce of Halifax writes convincingly of sea and ships, but his poetry carries the personal, insular emotion of one still unaware of immediates.' Kennedy later said, after reading Bruce's poetic responses, that a typographical error had resulted in 'immediates' replacing 'political immediacies'.

Back Road Farm

This house is built within a sheltering
Sweep of the hills. You will not find the sea
From attic windows; and the seasons bring
No lift and change of tide, here in the lee
Of the land's high windbreak, where the buffeting
Onshore wind is tripped on the mountain's knee.
No mist of blowing salt is flung to sting
The trusting flesh. You will not find the sea.

This property is private. Drifting rain
Beats on its shingles and its native stone;
The wind of August on its leaning grain
Is dark with shadow, and the leaves are blown
To a soft thunder. But the hills remain;
Their strength is certain and their purpose known.
Only at night, in the stillness, low and plain
You can hear the far deep rumor of sea on stone.

An Ear to the Ground

An ear to the ground—and wait—
You hear the chuckle and slap
Of chop in the surly strait
A thousand miles by the map?

Oh no; it is only a fault
Engrained in the rock of the mind;
Remembered grace to the halt,
Remembered sight to the blind.

Whatever the world becomes,
They will not leave you alone—
The old impersonal drums
Of leisurely surf on stone.

An echo, following still;
A silence, gathered and drowned
In tides of a restless will
To live again with the sound.

It's comfort in your virtue
And penance for your sins,
Till somewhere east of Cornwall
The smell of salts begins.

March Day: Windy

This day you wonder, finding nowhere quite
What you expect to find. The strident air
Surrounds you like a sea of sweeping light;
The hills and fields return you stare for stare.

Humpbacked and grim, the giant juniper
Bows down to scowl; across the crawling grass
Beyond, where the twin Balm o' Gileads were,
Two strangers halt and stiffen as you pass.

Something is altered here. The difference
Between you and the blowing world is thinned.
You turn to face the house, and common sense,
And see a woman shouldering the wind.

Turn to the barn, and see an old man leaning,
Intent, to hear those droning syllables—
Those phrases harsh and high, and wild with meaning,
Of shouted sound from granite-throated hills.

Orchards in the Woods

Red spruce and fir have crossed the broken lines
Where ragged fences ran; ground-juniper
Covers the sunny slope where currant bushes
Blackened their hanging clusters in green leaves.
Where oats and timothy moved like leaning water
Under the cloudy sweep of August wind,
The crop is stunted alders and tall ferns.

Above the cellar's crust of falling stone
Where timbered walls endured the treacherous
Traffic of frost and sunlight, nothing stands …
Under the wreckage of the vanished barn
A woodchuck burrows. Where the dooryard was,
The matted grass of years encloses now
Two horseshoes and a rusted wagon-tire.

Only the apple trees recall the dream
That flowered here — in love and sweat and growth,
Anger and longing. Tough and dark and wild,
Grown big of stump, rough in the bark and old,
They still put forth a light ironic bloom
Against the green utility of spruce.

Clearing and field and buildings gone to waste —
But in the fall, a gunner going home
will halt a moment, lift a hand to reach
One dusky branch above the crooked track,
And, thinking idly of his kitchen fire,
Bite to the small black shining seeds and learn
The taste of ninety seasons, hard and sweet.

The Mulgrave Road

If they stay they stay, if they go they go;
On the Mulgrave Road it's a choice you make.
There's an axe in the stump and a fork in the row
Or a bag to pick and a train to take.

Sandy was one of the wandering sort;
Not for adventure, not for play;
But a fellow that cut the taking short
And followed the earth for a season's pay.

It was just that his hardwood stand was gone
From the sidehill woodlot across the creek—
And he shipped on a tramp at West Saint John
For Boston, Georgetown and Martinique.

His hands were busy with sea and stone,
Timber and tractor, rope and bale.
The years grew short. And his grin was known
In Denver and Brandon, Spokane, Trail.

He knew Dundee and the Surrey Docks
And the wired shoulders of Vimey Ridge
As well as the road of gravel and rocks
From Grady's Place to the Iron Bridge.

You can see the rainclouds gather and pass
Over Hadley's Beach or the Artois plain;
And dust on the grass is dust on the grass
In Guysborough County or Port of Spain.

It was oar and crosscut, shovel and crank,
Hour by hour and year by year;
Till he heard, in a dory on Georges Bank,
Adventure calling, sudden and clear.

If they go they go, if they stay they stay;
But once in a hundred a man will pack
His clothes — and his habits — and roll away;
Or a lad with the wandering eye come back.

It was just that he knew, in his tranquil mind,
He was done with the habit of chance and change;
And his eyes were eager at last to find
Something different, something strange.

You can find him deep in his venture still,
The green oats growing, the young corn hoed —
Where the stumps are gone from a hardwood hill
By the turn of a creek on the Mulgrave Road.

Coast Farm

Hustling sheep to the barn, out of the squall, in April,
Shoulders hunched, hands in mackinaw pockets,
Numberless wisps of what he did and was
And learned to expect, and felt, and pondered over,
Drift in his moving flesh:

He walks in stubble
Trampling in damp earth and wet glistening stems,
And the dry rustle of last year's yellow oats
Lives in the senses; while the moment drifts
He sees, hears, feels the rush of wind and shadow,
Feels in his grip the scythe—

The scythe, the shoulder's ache and the clenched grip
On skinsmooth handles; and the moment fades—

Fades, and reshapens: his flex fingers crook
To the gripped jolt of oars. The falling swath
Is rolling groundswell; where an oatfield was,
The dark fleet glitter of next summer's herring
Gleams; till the shimmer wavers and is lost
(wet oilskin, blowing spray)
In the sodden fabric and the bite of rain.

Always the small swift thing that takes you backward;
The thing remembered, blurring in something else,
Next year, tomorrow. And the thing in that
Or the thing seen, heard, smelt, tasted, touched,
Turning again to now.

An old ewe blats:
Spring fencing, sheep to shear.

The coloured images
Move in a sea of sense, and waves of thought
March to the shore of mind.

Halting, he turns to lift one ranging glance
At raingrey water under a sea of cloud.

Disapproving Woman

The look she gives you is a tightened thread
Between the stitches of her spoken thought.
In the deft warning of her shaken head
A guilt is whispered, and a lesson taught.
The careful shadow of remembering doubt
Lives in her eyes, and with upright mind
She meets affliction: resolute, devout,
Never unkind and never wholly kind.

The years have given her all the years require:
Birch in the woodbox, credit at the store,
Comfort and friendship, work and food and fire;
But life has endless grief to answer for—
Death, and the sins of men and the blood's desire,
And muddy footprints on the kitchen floor.

Early Morning Landing

In daylight, there is life and living speech;
The constant grumble, the resilient splash
Of slow tide lifting on a slanted beach;
And blowing sunlight. And the measured flash
Of the sea marching ... But the beach and bay
Are vague as midnight now; in midnight thinned
At the sky's edge by the first hint of grey.
And calm as sleep before the morning wind.

Calmer than sleep. But the eyes lift to find
In the veiled night the faint recurring spark
Of a known beacon. And the listening mind
Wakes in the stillness; and the veil is stirred
By a dim ghost of sound—a far-off word
And the soft thump of rowlocks in the dark.

Girls in the Parlour

They have held funerals and weddings here.
And on the wall, in cardboard and dull gilt,
They keep the faces, bearded, stern, austere
Of men who cleared the place, and plowed and built—

And women: bold, shy, laughing, sensitive,
Or stiff with pride, in frills of lace and lawn,
Who came serenely to this house to live
And brought their girlhood with them, and are gone.

This is the room they held against the claims
Of earth and sead and time—the touch of grace.
And you can see them in their oval frames
In gowns of buttoned satin, and white lace.

Grey Ship Moving

I

She was built for the stylish South American run,
To haul smooth silk, on every kind of body,
Through the degrees to Rio and B.A.
Laid down at Belfast in Nineteen Thirty-nine,
Six hundred and forty feet of naked ship,
Twenty-five thousand gross, seventeen underdeck,
And fourteen thousand net;
Designed for comfort. (Look her up in Lloyds.)

But *Sappho* was never to house in her panelled cabins
The civilized holiday spirit of Park Lane.
Pender Street and Portage Avenue,
St. Clair and Barrington and the unnamed roads
From Musgrave to Boylston,
From Sand Lake to Kearney—
These were the thoroughfares that led to her hammocks,
Through the enlistment hut and basic training,
Through Bordon's dust and the mud of flat Debert;
And thus down to the long seawall at Halifax
Where she lay with her iron troopdecks ready and cold.

II

'Get going, Steve. They're yelling the second sitting.'
At five o'clock he had finally dropped asleep—
Three hours' grace from the nagging ache of knowing
The old life gone and the new one still unknown.
Now it would come—the smarting clutch of thought.
'Okay, Glen. I'll be there in a couple of shakes.
But you can't expect a Field Education jerk
To be quite as smart as the damned artillery infants.'

Down in the clutter of E-Deck the officers' mess
Was filling now for the second time that morning,

As Steve and Glen edged through the deck-long queue
Of Other Ranks lined up with their clattering mess-tins.
An impulse caught him: to jettison hat and pips,
Borrow a wedgie and join the grumbling line.

That's where I belong, with the clerk and the factory hand,
And the boys from the farms who never got past Grade Seven.
But what have they got for a bookish, near-sighted scribbler,
With a tentative foot on the door-step of middle age?
Books, and a place somewhere at battalion headquarters,
Lecturing, posting bulletins, reading the news.

The gripe stayed with him, back in the bunk-walled cabin
Tucked into *Sappho*'s middle to house a steward,
Polite, discreet, for the South American run—
Occupied now by four long-legged lieutenants:
Stephen Clare of Toronto, in Education;
Felix Lane, an exuberant engineer
Fresh from the apple-lands of the Okanagan;
An ordnance man, Jack Dunn, from the Eastern Townships,
And Glen Maguire, the gunner from Saskatoon.

Jack and Felix were out. The need for talk
Bothered his puzzling mind.
                                        'I'll tell you, Glen;
Down by the little harbour in Nova Scotia
You can see the humps in the grass where a Stephen Clare
Once built a vessel; a fore-and-aft three-master.
He cleared her for Africa one Thursday morning
And hasn't been heard from once in seventy years.
Great-uncle Steve. There must have been venturing blood
Somewhere among us. They couldn't find it in me.

> *Ah, Clare, you get along well with people,*
> *Or so it seems, if ever they get to know you.*
> *A little slow for a combat officer, what?*
> *Yes; not exactly in combat category.*

My own damn fault. I should never have gone to cities
And got myself tangled up in their easy living ...
Not that it's always been so filthy easy;
There's plenty of grief in fiddling advertising.
But it doesn't harden your body. The mind gets edgy.'

He found himself thinking back to a brown-walled office,
The telephone: 'No, can't make it for dinner, Margaret.'
And telling it all to Maguire. Thinking in speech.
Men as a general rule don't talk about women;
Not about women who share the days of their life.
Stephen was quiet and brief.
'The glow didn't last;
Two kids and a place to look after, and not much time,
With the office close to my mind, and the housework dull,
To think about being a man and woman together.'

It was odd to remember, here on a bunk at sea,
The onetime sequence of phrase and heading and layout;
The clear-eyed skill consumed in the changing task
Of selling assorted goods to a million neighbours,
Door-to-door through the *Herald, Gazette* and *Star*.
Adding a dash of pepper to lifeless words,
Kindling a glow in the virtues of disinfectant,
Taking the cold starch out of pink brassieres.

Steve caught himself. He had talked too much already;
The end of the story formed in his lively mind,
But he left it there. The words turned inward only:
'We came at last to be perfectly self-contained.
At least, I thought I was; till the moment came.
She was matter-of-fact as ice. And I'm damned if I know
Whether she wants me back in the end or not.
Boy, that was the minute that's running still in my throat;
That was the minute that stopped the perishing clock.'

They had grown together in three full days at sea
In the easy way men have when devious chance
Settles them close among an impersonal crowd.

Steve needn't have worried at setting his heart ajar;
Glen bothered never at all about inward matters.
'Yes, women are queer. The one I want's in England—
I came over in Forty, you know; went back for the pips—
Brings me tea in the morning. We might get married.
Too much to finish up first. I'll play you again.'

He straightened the board they had pencilled on wrinkled paper
And set up the checkers—Canadian pennies and dimes.
Steve envied him now—not youth and obvious courage,
But careless trust in the hour, faith in the day,
Belief in the minute—and independence of all.

Felix came in, full of his own good humour,
And hauled himself into a blanketed upper bunk.
'I'm talent scouting; we're due for a ship's concert;
Boy, but the stuff we've found—there's a little Wren—'

The picture carried him back to a Saturday night,
A girl from somewhere, heading for somewhere else,
And a hotel room in Brockville. Glen was bored.
'Put it on paper. We heard that story before.'

The tiresome voice ran on, evoking an image
Of young desire and casual passion remembered.
Steve jumped at a threatening penny and cursed in his mind,
Chilled at the commonplace story beyond all reason;
Then grinned as he thought:
'Hell, it's just that I'm envious,
Never having been much of a hand with women,
And the time getting past for it now.'

At dinner time, by the steel dispensary door
He heard Lane's voice, to the harassed medical sergeant:
'I don't care how many patients; this man's sick;
He's been here three times and you give him salts and water—
I'm staying here till the bloody M.O. sees him.'

Yes, Lane will think of his men, careful and thorough,
Till a spandau gets him, somewhere beyond Falaise.

III

The sheen of linen, the glow of lamps on silver,
Had never graced a dining saloon in *Sappho*.
Here where a mellow light was meant to linger
Over white cloth and cognac and shining hair,
Two thousand Other Ranks in khaki and blue
Crowded together on benches, hunched on tables,
Joking and jamming, waiting for Felix Lane.

He kept them anxious only a careful minute,
Till the green curtains moved, and through a door
Designed to lead warm flesh to well-fed living,
Came Sandra March, in a gown of cinnamon red.
Section Officer March, the listing called her;
Bound overseas to the Midland bomber stations,
Away from Carnegie Hall and the concert crowds
Of twenty cities from Montreal to Frisco.
And singing now, to the notes of an old piano
Played by the LAC from Thetford Mines:
'Sweetheart' and 'Blackbird' and 'Sierra Sue',
Faithful and clear, above the whispered anthem
Of this grey ship and the long Atlantic seas …

And now we listen to Colin Somers of Margate,
Onetime glee-club singer and draper's assistant,
England-bound from the training fields of Texas:
'Old Man River' and 'Wandering the King's Highway'.
And laugh with tall Jack Dunn, well coached by Felix,
Producing underwear out of an empty hat.

And nothing is hackneyed or banal; Steve knew it was good
As a string quartette and a husky baritone voice
Strummed into 'Shanty Town' and 'Five Foot Two'.

That night, in the cabin alone, he tried to capture
With hesitant pencil the happy and pensive spirit
That opened here at the intimate touch of music
And the wings of laughing sound;
Turning — a mental adventure — to rhythm and verse
The skill he had learned in the use and value of words;
And thought: 'It's a bit overdone; a bit too dramatic.
But still — not far from the truth. Not far from the truth.'

The sense moved in him at least of a new task done,
A new road opened along the crags of the mind:

> *A young voice calls in true and wistful song,*
> *Simple as woodlands under windy rain;*
> *Clear as December stars, and gently strong*
> *As amber light on fields of August grain.*
> *Here we have felt the long compelling grip*
> *Of tribal wonder. They have woven a spell*
> *In this grey messdeck of a throbbing ship*
> *Shouldering down the North Atlantic swell.*
> *The bow is drawn; the fingers move to seek*
> *Remembered tones of rock and earth and sky,*
> *Remembered traceries of crawling fire.*
> *And through the violin's persuasive cry*
> *Once more and once again the straining creak*
> *Of steel and wood and weather-tightened wire.*

IV

On the seventh night Steve woke in the deadly hours
That bridge the middle dark; and lay in his blankets,
Cradled now in the gentle roll of *Sappho*
Going her charted way in a quartering sea.
Maguire and Dunn snored softly, deeply asleep;
Felix had not returned from a C-Deck crap game;
The cabin door knocked lightly against its hook
Of polished brass, ajar to the roll of the ship.

He was fully awake, a question stirring his mind
Like the formless words of an unrecalled quotation.
Restless, he slipped from the bunk, pulled on a trenchcoat
And quietly sidled into the dusky passage.

Not far away a sleepy security guard
Lounged with his back to the slowly swaying wall.
Stephen approached and offered a cigarette,
Grateful for someone to talk to. 'Thanks; have a light?'
He studied the youngster, friendly and open as daylight.

'It sure gets lonesome, nights, with nothing to do
But hang around here for something that never happens.'

The question in Stephen's mind began to emerge.
For more than a week he had wondered and worried and thought—
While his body moved automatically through the routine
Of morning and noontime and midnight, waking and sleep—
Of himself alone, his dreams and his wife and his children.
Now at this lightless hour one thing was clear:
On this grey ship he was one—and one of six thousand.
Six thousand venturing men and twoscore women,
Each one a person, each with his own close dreams,
Vague as the clouds, or bright as a glistening star.

'Sir? Oh … Talbot's my name; from the Lakehead;
They christened me Wilbur. For God's sake call me Bill.
Worked at the elevators around Ford William
Till I got to be army age; and then I enlisted—
Not sorry, either; the doing's got to be done.'

He halted a moment, laughing; a bit embarrassed
At talking this way, chattering, shooting a line.

'There was this about it; you can't stay out of the show.
When it's over I'm going to have a shot at Toronto;
There's a job in a hardware store. I could learn the business.'

You can't stay out of the show. No choice in the matter.
You can't stay out of the show. And what was the answer,
Whatever the simple or intricate threads of impulse
Close-woven in secret life; whatever the task;
That was the answer, in verdict simple and final,
For all who crossed the impersonal sea with *Sappho*.

He quietly asked: 'How old are you, Bill?' 'Nineteen.
Cripes'—with a laugh—'I'll be twenty-two at least
When we get this job cleaned up. Old man with a crutch.'
The laugh was there, but the words not all in fun.
Steve grinned from the ancient peak of his thirty-seven.
And later on Bill got his crutch; at Breskens.

V

They woke next day to unfamiliar stillness,
Gathered on deck to find the rainwet rail
Running no longer past a moving sea.
Fog was a distant veil, but through its pallor
Loomed the vague darker folds of factory smoke,
And sharper, jutting from the drab horizon,
The stilted symmetry of channel flak-towers.

'Well, then, we've made it; holding for the tide;'
Glen moved away, laughing among the crowd
Of noisy voyagers in blue and khaki.

Steve strained his eyes toward the distant screen
Of shadowy fog and smoke and creeping cloud.
Fawn-coloured water grumbled and slapped at *Sappho*:
A thousand gulls, muttering, veering, crying,
Circled and held position, riding the wind.
Morning went by, and the ebb tide turned to flood.

Behind the fog lay all the towns of England,
And quietness lived at last in Stephen's heart.

For no accountable cause, at no fixed hour,
The dark cloak fell away; as *Sappho*'s chain
Came clanking up out of the tidal murk
And the grey ship moved again on the channel tide
His heart went with her, light with the dream of life.
He could feel at last all living as endless venture,
Laughter and grief, indifference, power and pain.

The grey ship moved; and in his answering spirit
The pride, the song, the blood of an ancient race
Welled up in infinite sureness to blend with its own.

The clock had started again.
                                        And at that moment
A woman wrote on a blue and flimsy form
The forthright words of passion she could not say —
The ardent words reborn in a dream rekindled
Out of a pattern sharp with the colour of living;
The years of success and desire, of failure and love.

Lake Superior Coast: Train Window

East of the port, the gaunt Euclidian town
At the edge of the prairie sky, at the venturous end
Of the sea's last traffic with the climbing land—
You come to the hills. The spruce and rock steep down

To the mountain beach. Inlet and channel and reef
Return, in the slow dance of land's turning;
Shadowed and clear and dark in the desolate raining
Of lost and shadowy light, and the lost brief

Moment; flashed and repeated in the drumming wheels.
Repeat ... repeat ... repeat; the flashing earth
Streams in its rhythm; and the moment's breath
Is time's deliberate breath. The wheeling hills

Drift with its tide ... The hills and the quilted flock
Of the sky, and a gull, remotely flying
And stilled in flight ...
                                        Time, and the granite flowing
Of stonegrey water and precambrian rock.

Late Marriage

Plates on her cupboard shelves gleam in the pale
Thin plates of sunlight. Settling in the stove
Hardwood and fire make whispering talk: and in
The mind's long room the subtle patterns move:
Old summers, distant falls, the green of springs ...
Forgotten hills, a child with soundless voice
Singing, and August fields. The dream is caught
And webbed and wedded to them, and the choice
Not hers but Time's ... They wake and drift and blend
Persistent, tenuous, frail as smoke and thin
As sunlight ... But the mind is suddenly still:
The porch door opens now and he comes in.
Slowly, and smiling. And she cannot tell
Which arrow pierces her — the dream that lies
Between them, or the mouth's half-rueful twitch —
Or his hands, or the boyishness around his eyes.

Tidehead

Never make it plain
That in your inner knowing
With tidesweep and rain
You see a likeness growing.

When blood has its way
From the same burdened mother,
Do you need to say
Your brother is your brother?

Enough then to know
Is kinship without saying
For the long grey flow
And the salt kelp straying;

Enough to have seen —
The marsh a moist blotter,
And the slick wet green
Of eelgrass at low water.

Return and Introduction

I

Eight years or ten are time enough to lay
Uneasy change along the rutted track;
Ploughed fields are bush, and russet roofs are grey,
And time has moved the wagon and the stack.
Or is it only that remembering eyes,
Once keen to spring's return and summer's going,
Tricked by the town's insistent symmetries
Have lost their old discernment, never knowing?

Two roads go hither, and two hills are thrust
Into the shining of a double sun;
And I—uncertain if the earthy crust
Of sober truth envelops either one—
Go aimless, questioning in which of these
Lives the lost friendliness I came to seize.

II

He was polite to strangers, but his mind
Was fixed on other matters and his pride
Walked in the future privately, to find
A cavalier with triumph in his stride.
I, who am nice to strangers, meet him so:
Go reaching back to beach and field and hill
Without regret or jubilance, to know
The boy who looked beyond tomorrow still.

Wordless, I question him: And is your thought
Familiar with this bearing and this face?
Does this design the quickening years have wrought
Wake no return of time, no hint of place?
Not yet has any fire of greeting starred
The grave politeness in his calm regard.

Spirit of a Province

How shall a word, in changing sound, express
A thing grown tangible through furrowed clay;
Through grasses weaving upward; and the grey
Far-stretching autumn hills? The rugged stress
Of sea on stone may give you wit to guess—
No more than that—this care for yesterday
And vision of tomorrow; and the spray
May point your wonder to its inwardness.

But words avail not. If you still must know,
Mark how in any land we turn to see
Some new device, some truth of nature's law
Brought to man's use in magnified degree,
And say: 'It minds me of a thing I saw
In Yarmouth or in Sydney—years ago'.

The Standing Woods

I

A hundred years ago a man still living
Might have recalled the drift of something said
In his own youth, and held the key to guess
Why James and Catherine sailed from Aberdeen.
But memory's coin is action; and the act
Is all there is, simple and smooth and bare,
Motive and impulse fused within its metal.

We have no way of knowing; the act is bare.
Nor do we know what town or settlement
In that far county's eighty parishes
Knew them as children; more than sixty miles
Of coast run north and west through Peterhead,
And the wide shire runs westward to the hills
That skirt the Grampians. And the name is common.

We only know they sailed from Aberdeen
With kindred of their blood, and made a landfall,
And chopped a clearing on this wooded coast.

The axe, the saw, the drawknife and the froe;
Chisel and auger, shaving-horse and adze ...
Conceived in sweat the settlements began
Between the water and the standing woods.

Of hand-sawn lumber joined with hardwood logs,
In daylight spared from stump-entangled earth,
(Between May seeding and September mowing,
After the threshing and before the frost)
They raised their houses based on native stone.

The axe, the hoe, the reaping-hook, the scythe ...
And breeds of men. On that impersonal shore

Where the sea curls on Nova Scotia's edge
The Celt and Saxon met to fashion living;
Motive and impulse fusing in the act
That brought them; crusty Scots whom Cumberland
Dressed in red coats and fed and sent away
To keep them off the back of George the Third;
English and Irish, English and more Scots.

The loyalists landed, harried from the States
By pride and conscience and another George;
And still more Scotsmen; crofters from the west,
Stripped of their holdings by the cautious lairds—
Their dun fields on the hills above the Clyde.

(The cautious lairds, careful and practical,
Viewing the textile trade and knowing wool
A far more likely crop than men and women) ...

This was the coast where James and Catherine settled
With John, their infant son; and in this land
Richard and Christopher and young Maria
were born to live and marry; a stone or two
Record their chiselled names. (But flesh and blood
In Boylston, Gloucester, Wilmington, New Glasgow,
San Bernardino, Halifax, New York,
Trace in the veins a tenuous chronicle
More eloquent than memory or stone.)

Together on their strips of measured earth
The strength of men was joined in common labour;
To pull the stumps and burn the reddening brush
And drive their clearings inward from the sea.

Thus James began to sow his living here,
In rugged ground, clearing the rough fields
And planting life. For six hard-driving years
His hands were busy with the flashing axe.

What common dreams were his of larger living
Beyond the simplest needs of night and day
We have no way of knowing. The act is bare.

There is no way of knowing. We only know
He joined his neighbours in the standing woods
And chopped; and died beneath a crashing tree.

II

The axe, the plough, the tiller and the sail;
The slow and unregarded growth of time ...
If a young man had left the changing coast
In those first days of crude and stubborn work
And journeyed homeward after fifty years
To mark the difference ... But the sum of truth
Is scattered now in scraps and vestiges,
The track of action, not translatable:
Scars in a grassy field, a rusting anchor,
And men and women, continents apart,
With bloodlines tracing to a distant beach.

A certain broadened living must have grown
Around the settlements. In fifty years
The pasture lands had lost their choking brush,
The grey stumps rotted from the planted fields,
The saddle-path become a wagon-track,
Rutted with mud and holed with rising frost.

We know that in the spring they left the land
And took to whaleboats—setting their dark nets
In the home bay for mackerel; sailing forth
On distant channels when the schooling fish
Followed the seasons north.
Between the ports
The trading schooners plied the routes of life,
Before the railway came, before the steamer

Was common on the coast. With barrelled fish
And timber loaded in their slippery holds
They cleared the customs, sailed, and reappeared
With flour and leather, nails and rope and salt.

The years were marching; in the course of years
Another James had grown to dig and chop
And hold a whaleboat on her labouring course—
A grandson of the man from Aberdeen.
This younger James and Charles were Richard's sons;
But it was Charles who worked the growing farm,
Tended the barn, looked to the horse and cattle,
Planted and reaped and kept to the home beach.

(Did James the elder fish the grey North Sea
From landings on the sandy shores of Mar?)

In the young James another impulse worked.
Perhaps the dream, the spirit of this land,
The dream that never shaped itself in speech,
Was quickened in him in a moment kept
Unsold for labour in the store of time.

The foot of Richard's land dropped to a harbour
Channelled behind a wooded spit of beach
By the long action of recurring tide.
James had a vessel built and fitted there,
And launched her at high water. No one knows
The journeys of that small forgotten ship.
(But Will recalled her name, the *J.J. Marshall.*)
He may have sailed her in the coastal trade,
But all we surely know is that the *Marshall*
Drops out of memory; James appears again
Sailing another craft, the *Princess Dagmar.*

In the dark vaults of some old custom house
Dim volumes may record in faded ink
The entries that would give these voyages

A dated clarity. But it scarcely matters;
The tale is in the act. The act is bare.

He knew the lore of water, bought a ship
For Western Ocean work, and signed a crew
From settlements along the quiet shore.

What part of this was shrewd and careful trade
And what part simple venture? No one knows.

We only know the vessel weighed and sailed,
And headed east, bound for Sierra Leone,
And cleared the coast and vanished without trace.

III

There was a continuity in this land;
A continuity and a branching out.
Children and grandchildren of the first James—
Of Richard, Christopher, Maria, John—
Settled nearby, but always in the end
Most of them moved away; married and moved
Or suddenly found the growing land too crowded
And drifted, close and far, to meet their fortune—
The long unchanging destiny of change.

But the first land was never left untended.
James, Richard, Charles and Will, four generations,
Worked in its earth and in its winter woods
And off its windy beach.
Until the call
Of urgent blood, or restless enterprise,
While Charles was still a man of middle years,
Awoke in Will the need to pack and go.

(Did one considered voice, in Aberdeen,
Give quiet counsel, eighty years before?)

Now, to the boy who used to ask and listen,
Learning of Will the savour of past days
Long after these New England years were ended,
Boston is just a city on the coast,
A junction point between New York and Maine.
But in that talk beside the kitchen fire,
On winter nights, a brief enchantment ran —
Austen and Stone's Museum, Tremont Temple,
Charlestown and Faneuil Hall and Phillips Brooks,
Mike Kelly sliding home ... the great John L ...

Will worked in Boston at the trade he knew
From practice with his native spruce and birch,
Shaping the wood for desk and cabinet,
Learning the ways of rosewood and veneer.
(Long after, he could watch a white pine grow,
Chop it at last, and from the seasoned lumber,
Construct a lap-streak boat with his own hands.)

He married there a dark-haired girl from home,
And fathered children; with a hundred others
From the home coast, the pattern of their lives
Was cut to fit the manner of the States.

There is a question here, a paradox;
For Will had more than most, in heart and talent,
Of those who leave ancestral settlements
To forge a living elsewhere. He came back —
Back to the fields, the woodlots and the beach.

Were city streets too crowded, too intense,
Too shaken with a jostling and a clamour,
After the first flush of the Boston years?
Too fertile with the seeds of weariness,
Too distant from the lift of boyhood hills?

Or was it something else, an inner knowing
That this new venture was already old,

That fresh horizons beckoned here no more,
But opened from the purlieus of his birth?

Though well-remembered voices haunt us yet,
These are the answers no one ever knows.

We only know he worked the place again,
Relearned the ways of harrow, scythe and plough,
Fished for the mackerel that never ran,
The herring that ran silver in the nets,
And urged his children not to think of home—
To fix their dreams on getting off this land,
Where life was straitly bounded by hard work,
And little money, and a shortened view.

Perhaps that was the measure of their venture—
Will and his dark-haired girl—the chance of life,
Achievement, failure, dreams and children living ...
The venture promised in the flesh renewed.

We only know that at his rowboat's oars,
Timed to the lurch and sway of buoyant swell,
His hands were deft and ready, and his face
Cleared of all conflict in the running wind.

IV

The house is empty now, the old fields tilled
By thrifty neighbours of another name;
And those who lived within it scattered far
Across the reaches of a continent;
In Edmonton, Saskatchewan, Detroit,
Toronto and the Californian hills ...

Study and work and marriage, love and anger,
The common gaiety and the unshared dark,
Lived with and dealt with in the changing ways
The generations fashioned in their blood.

A word is spoken; in the measured tone
Is there one turning of a common sound,
One echo of a long-forgotten voice
That called across the Nova Scotian beach?

The pencil moves, and in the shorthand stroke
Does one lost movement live, one trick of touch,
One grace that quickened to the spindle's rhythm,
In some long vanished room in Aberdeen?

One question, for the first who landed here,
For all who laboured in the standing woods,
And planted life and sent their flesh afar:

What twist of Devon speech is heard in Butte?
What song that echoed once along the Clyde
Is half-remembered on the Erie shore?

(Stone fences clamber still, beyond Dunoon,
Where the cock-pheasant calls from the yellow gorse,
And narrow and dark in its loch the resilient sea
Goes curving home to the steep low heart of the hills.)

The records crumble; letters in the dust;
A story living awhile in old men's minds,
And fading slowly in the loft of time;
Smoke from the fires of action kindled here,
Kindled and turned to ash and lit again,
And blown to flame by the long winds of blood;
Motive and impulse fusing in the act,
And the act lost to conscious memory,
To find renewal in the flesh renewed.

The records fade. And it will be enough
To know, in Montreal or New South Wales,
Or anywhere, a hundred years from now,
A young man scrawling on the careless page:
'Originally, we came from Nova Scotia;

A long time back, it was, and no one knows
Just why they left the place, and no one knows
Just where it was — Guysborough or Halifax —
One of the counties on the Eastern Shore.'

He will not wonder much about the past,
Concerned in this day's work, tomorrow's work,
The dream that looks beyond tomorrow's edge …
Now and again a brief and aimless thought,
Once in a while, perhaps, a curious word,
A casual question and a glancing back
To scan the index of a dimming story.

Then let him turn again, as I do now,
A traveller in the standing woods of time,
Alone, but not entirely alone …

Upstairs Room

Six days a week he never saw this room
To see it. Winter and summer, spring and fall,
He would be up and out in the grey loom
Of early daylight. Bed and floor and wall
Were shapes and dreams and shadows. And at night
After the stonedrag, harrow, axe and hoe,
When he went up again the day's last light
Was emptied from it, and the lamp turned low ...

Only on Sunday mornings. That was when,
The barnwork finished, he would go upstairs
To change, at leisure. He would see it then:
This odd familiar place: its curious chairs,
And wall, rose-figured; and the sun that crept,
Slowly, on floor and bedspread. And its worn
Hooked mats, and curtains. This was where he slept.
And where (someone had told him) he was born.

Afterword

My father always carried fat, black, soft-leaded pencils in an inside breast pocket of his suit coat. The words *Canadian Press*, in silver letters, were stamped into each pencil, and the tips of the lead were as sharp as pins. It's his poetry and fiction that preserve his memory, but older newspapermen across the country still know that it was to Canadian Press, the national news-gathering agency, that he sold his days and sweat. Mostly in Toronto, he worked hard, long hours for CP, hard, long years; and rose to become its General Manager. Among many other things there, he was the ruler and watchdog over grammar, spelling and copy style throughout CP's empire. After his retirement and, in 1971, his death, CP's standards of literacy declined, slowly but drastically.

Others who cared about correct prose in daily journalism recognized him as an authority and, while preparing style guides for their own newspapers, consulted him. At home, too, his passion for correct English usage hovered on the pleasant side of pedantry. He was the first person I ever heard fume over what has now become the ubiquitous misuse of 'hopefully'. When arguments arose over the meaning of a word, or the proper uses of 'which' and 'that' (a distinction I have not mastered to this day), he'd impatiently get up from his chesterfield and march over to the *Oxford English Dictionary* or *Fowler's English Usage*. Then he'd read aloud the appropriate scripture, and that would settle that. He actually read *Fowler* for pleasure.

Since he spent so much of his working life at CP, it used to puzzle me that so little of the newspaperman was evident in his poetry. 'Grey Ship Moving' (1945), his epic about a troop-ship sailing from Halifax ('where she lay with her iron troopdecks ready and cold') did result from journalistic experience. And 'Words Are Never Enough' was partly about a fine, continuing, news story of his young manhood, the men of the schooner *Bluenose*. But specific references to the experience of being in the news business, though they're sometimes the meat of his fiction, rarely pop up in his poetry.

But back to the black pencils. I remember the silky lining of his suit coats, and their smell, the smell of a man who had worked hard all day. His staff worked in their shirtsleeves but he always wore his suit coat at CP, even on the hottest days. The smell of his jacket in our front-hall closet said he was tired and, after supper, he'd lie down on his chesterfield and sleep. Then he'd get up, fetch a couple of those pencils, lie down on his back again, hold a pad of soft copy paper on his stomach — and start to write. Once, while my brothers and I were flat on our stomachs reading the daily comics and bickering and chattering, my mother called us out to the kitchen. She said, 'I wish you'd be more quiet, I think your father's writing a novel.' He'd been writing it in exactly that fashion for seven years. It was *The Channel Shore*.

The pencils, however, were only the most tangible link between CP and his creative writing. Though his news work provided few images for his poetry — and maybe the poetry was an escape from the other — he believed good news writing and good poetry had things in common: precision, economy, order, the search for the exact right word. There was another connection. His work on the chesterfield turned him into a successful poet and novelist, and this helped him in his work downtown. It gained him respect, not only at CP but on newspapers across the country. He actually did what so many news people merely yearn to do. He became a creative writer.

The pencils served him till the end. His memory had started to play tricks on him. He began to take notes to remind himself of things he'd promised to do, and to record what was happening to him. Even on the day before he died, he was jotting things down in that familiar, black, greasy lead. He was still a reporter and, in his failing heart, still a poet.

Harry Bruce
Halifax, Nova Scotia

About Charles Bruce

Charles Tory Bruce was born in Port Shoreham, Nova Scotia, on May 11, 1906. He was the son of a farmer-fisherman and his mother had been a schoolteacher. His first poems were published in the *North Sydney Herald*, a daily newspaper, and *The Family Herald*, a weekly. In 1927—the year he graduated from Mount Allison University in Sackville, New Brunswick—he privately published his first collection of poems, *Wild Apples*. That same year he worked as a reporter for the *Halifax Chronicle* before joining the Canadian Press. In 1928, he married Agnes King, with whom he had three sons.

Bruce published his second book of poems, *Tomorrow's Tide*, in 1932. The following year, he was transferred to CP's Toronto office where he became general news editor in 1937. Bruce served as war correspondent for CP from 1943 to 1944, stationed in New York and later London, England. In 1944, he was reported missing for several days after his Royal Canadian Airforce plane crash-landed in Belgium following an ill-fated airborne assault. He showed up in his London office to discover one of his colleagues writing his obituary.

After the war, Bruce returned to Canada where was appointed General Superintendent, the second-highest position in the CP hierarchy. Bruce wrote the original CP stylebook, the bible of journalistic prose. ('The news report', his company once wrote, 'gained character from [Bruce's] insistence that style rules are not a straightjacket to curb originality.') Between 1941 and 1947, Bruce published three more books of poetry, and, in 1951, he gained a wide readership with *The Mulgrave Road*, which won the Governor General's Award for Poetry. In 1952, his former university awarded him with an honorary doctorate of letters.

Bruce published only one novel, *The Channel Shore*, in 1954, and in 1959 published a collection of linked short stories, *The Township of Time*. He retired from CP in 1963, and devoted his final years to researching two projects, a novel related to the Second World War, which was never finished, and a history of the Southam newspaper empire, which he published in 1968 under the title *News and the Southams*. Bruce died in his sleep in 1971, at the age of sixty-five.

Bibliography

POETRY

Wild Apples (Tribune Press, 1927)
Tomorrow's Tide (Macmillan Company, 1932)
Personal Note (Ryerson Press, 1941)
Grey Ship Moving (Ryerson Press, 1945)
The Flowing Summer (Ryerson Press, 1947)
The Mulgrave Road (Macmillan, 1951)

FICTION

The Channel Shore (Macmillan, 1954)
The Township of Time (Macmillan, 1959)

NON-FICTION

News and the Southams (Macmillan, 1968)

HONOURS

Governor General's Literary Award for Poetry, 1951